The New Diabetes Recipe Book

Cook with Simple, Tasty and Wholesome ingredients

Evelin Turk

Table of Contents

Garbanzo Bean, Spinach, And Feta Tabbouleh

Servings: 4

Ingredients:

1 cup water

3⁄4 cup uncooked fine-grind bulgur

1 teaspoon grated lemon zest

3 tablespoons lemon juice

1 tablespoon extra virgin olive oil

1 small garlic clove, crushed through a press

1⁄2 teaspoon kosher salt

1⁄8 teaspoon freshly ground pepper

1 cup grape tomatoes, halved

1⁄2 hothouse (English) cucumber, chopped

1 (15-ounce) can no-salt-added garbanzo beans, rinsed and drained

1⁄2 cup chopped fresh Italian parsley

1⁄4 cup chopped fresh mint

2 cups loosely packed fresh baby spinach

1 ounce finely crumbled feta cheese (about ¼ cup)

Directions:

1. Pour the water in a small saucepan and bring to a boil over high heat. Remove from the heat and add the bulgur. Cover and let stand until the water is absorbed, 25 minutes.

2. Meanwhile, whisk together the lemon zest, lemon juice, oil, garlic, salt, and pepper in a large bowl. Add the bulgur and stir to combine. Let stand to cool to room temperature, stirring occasionally. Stir in the tomatoes, cucumber, beans, parsley, and mint. Toss in the spinach and feta just before serving. Serve at room temperature or chilled. The salad tastes best on the day it is made, but it can be refrigerated, covered, for up to 2 days.

Nutrition Info:

45 g carb, 272 cal, 6 g fat, 2 g sat fat, 6 mg chol, 10 g fib, 11 g pro, 257 mg sod • Carb Choices: 21/2; Exchanges: 2 starch, 1 veg, 1 plant- based protein, 1 fat

Garbanzo Picadillo

Servings: 6

Ingredients:

2 teaspoons extra virgin olive oil

1 medium onion, chopped

2 garlic cloves, minced

2 teaspoons ground cumin

1 teaspoon ground coriander

1/2 teaspoon kosher salt

1/4 teaspoon freshly ground pepper

1/4 teaspoon ground cinnamon

Pinch of ground cayenne

2 cups Vegetable Stock or low-sodium vegetable broth

2 (14 1/2-ounce) cans no-salt-added diced tomatoes

2 (15-ounce) cans no-salt-added garbanzo beans, rinsed and drained

1/4 cup golden raisins

2 tablespoons capers, rinsed and drained

2 tablespoons no-salt-added tomato paste

2 medium zucchinis, chopped

1 tablespoon honey

1 tablespoon sherry vinegar or white wine vinegar

Chopped fresh cilantro

Directions:

1. Heat a large saucepan over medium heat. Add the oil and tilt the pan to coat the bottom evenly. Add the onion and cook, stirring often, until softened, 5 minutes. Add the garlic, cumin, coriander, salt, pepper, cinnamon, and cayenne and cook, stirring constantly, until fragrant, 30 seconds. Add the stock, tomatoes, beans, raisins, capers, and tomato paste and bring to a boil over high heat.

2. Cover, reduce the heat to low, and simmer until the stew is slightly thickened, about 20 minutes. Add the zucchini and cook until just crisp- tender, about 3 minutes longer. Remove from the heat and stir in the honey and vinegar.

3. Ladle the stew evenly into 6 bowls, sprinkle with the cilantro, and serve at once. The stew can be refrigerated, covered, for up to 4 days or frozen for up to 3 months.

Nutrition Info:

42 g carb, 252 cal, 3 g fat, 0 g sat fat, 0 mg chol, 9 g fib, 11 g pro, 324 mg sod • Carb Choices: 3; Exchanges: 2 starch, 2 veg, 1 plant-based protein

Quinoa, Zucchini, And Mint Salad

Servings: 6

Ingredients:

1 1/2 cups water

1 cup quinoa, rinsed

3/4 teaspoon kosher salt, divided

1 teaspoon grated lime zest

2 tablespoons lime juice

1 1/2 tablespoons extra virgin olive oil

1/4 teaspoon freshly ground pepper

2 small zucchinis, quartered lengthwise and thinly sliced

2 tablespoons chopped fresh mint

2 tablespoons pine nuts, toasted

Directions:

1. Combine the water, quinoa, and 1/2 teaspoon of the salt in a medium saucepan and bring to a boil over high heat. Reduce the heat to low, cover, and simmer until the quinoa is tender, 12 to 15 minutes. Drain and keep warm.

2. Meanwhile, whisk together the lime zest, lime juice, oil, remaining 1/4 teaspoon salt, and the pepper in a large bowl. Stir in the hot cooked quinoa and let stand to cool to room temperature, stirring occasionally.

3. Add the zucchini and mint and stir to combine. Stir in the pine nuts just before serving. Serve at room temperature or chilled. The salad tastes best on the day it is made.

Nutrition Info:

22 g carb, 165 cal, 7 g fat, 1 g sat fat, 0 mg chol, 2 g fib, 5 g pro, 151 mg sod • Carb Choices: 1 1/2; Exchanges: 1 starch, 1 veg, 1 fat

Quinoa Salad with Mango, Orange, And Basil

Servings: 6

Ingredients:

1 1/2 cups water

1 cup quinoa, rinsed

3/4 teaspoon kosher salt, divided

2 teaspoons grated orange zest

3 tablespoons orange juice

2 tablespoons lime juice

1 1/2 tablespoons extra virgin olive oil

1 jalapeño, seeded and chopped

1 garlic clove, minced

1 mango, peeled, pitted, and chopped

1/4 cup chopped fresh basil

Directions:

1. Combine the water, quinoa, and 1/2 teaspoon of the salt in a medium saucepan and bring to a boil over high heat. Reduce the heat to low, cover, and simmer until the quinoa is tender, 12 to 15 minutes. Drain and keep warm.

2. Meanwhile, combine the orange zest, orange juice, lime juice, oil, jalapeño, garlic, and remaining 1/4 teaspoon salt in a blender and process until pureed. Transfer to a large bowl. Stir in the hot cooked quinoa and let stand to cool to room temperature, stirring occasionally.

3. Add the mango and basil to the quinoa mixture and stir to combine. Serve at room temperature or chilled. The salad tastes best on the day it is made.

Nutrition Info:

26 g carb, 162 cal, 5 g fat, 1 g sat fat, 0 mg chol, 2 g fib, 4 g pro, 147 mg sod • Carb Choices: 2; Exchanges: 1 1/2 starch, 1/2 fruit, 1 fat

Grilled Chicken Salad with Miso-basil Dressing

Servings: 4

Ingredients:

2 tablespoons white miso paste

2 tablespoons cold water

2 tablespoons rice vinegar

1 tablespoon plus 1/2 teaspoon canola oil

2 teaspoons grated fresh ginger

1/2 teaspoon chili-garlic paste

4 (4-ounce) boneless skinless chicken breasts

6 cups loosely packed torn romaine lettuce

1 cup cherry tomatoes, halved

1/2 large hothouse (English) cucumber, thinly sliced

1/4 cup thinly sliced red onion

2 tablespoons chopped fresh basil

Directions:

1. Prepare the grill or heat a large grill pan over medium-high heat.

2. Whisk together the miso, water, vinegar, 1 tablespoon of the oil, ginger, and chili-garlic paste in a small bowl. Spoon 2 tablespoons of the miso mixture into a shallow dish. Add the chicken and turn to coat. Let stand at room temperature for 15 minutes.

3. Brush the grill rack or grill pan with the remaining 1/2 teaspoon oil. Remove the chicken from the marinade and discard the marinade. Grill the chicken, turning often, until the juices of the chicken run clear, 8 to 10 minutes.

4. Meanwhile, combine the lettuce, tomatoes, cucumber, and onion in a large bowl. Stir the basil into the remaining miso mixture. Drizzle the salad with 2 tablespoons of the miso mixture and toss to coat. Divide the salad evenly among 4 plates. Top each salad with a chicken breast. Drizzle the chicken evenly with the remaining miso mixture. Serve at once.

Nutrition Info:

9 g carb, 203 cal, 7 g fat, 1 g sat fat, 63 mg chol, 4 g fib, 26 g pro, 334 mg sod • Carb Choices: 1/2; Exchanges: 1 veg, 3 lean protein, 1 fat

Carrots And Fennel Braised with White Wine And Garlic

Servings: 4

Ingredients:

1 medium bulb fennel

2 teaspoons extra virgin olive oil

2 garlic cloves, minced

1/2 teaspoon fennel seeds

8 ounces carrots, peeled and cut into 1/2-inch-thick sticks

1/2 cup dry white wine

3/4 teaspoon kosher salt

1 teaspoon lemon juice

Directions:

1. Trim the tough outer stalks from the fennel. Cut the fennel bulb in half vertically and cut away and discard the core. Cut each half lengthwise into 1/4-inch slices.

2. Heat a large nonstick skillet over medium heat. Add the oil and tilt the pan to coat the bottom evenly. Add the garlic and fennel seeds and cook, stirring constantly, until fragrant, 30 seconds. Add the fennel bulb, carrots, wine, and salt and bring to a boil over high heat. Reduce the heat to low, cover, and simmer until the vegetables are tender, 10 minutes. Uncover and cook until most of the liquid has evaporated, 2 minutes. Remove from the heat and stir in the lemon juice. Spoon the vegetables into a serving dish and serve at once.

Nutrition Info:

10 g carb, 86 cal, 3 g fat, 0 g sat fat, 0 mg chol, 3 g fib, 1 g pro, 276 mg sod • Carb Choices: 1/2; Exchanges: 2 veg, 1/2 fat

Dried Apricot–pecan Stuffing

Servings: 8

Ingredients:

6 cups 1/2-inch whole wheat bread cubes

3 teaspoons extra virgin olive oil, divided

1 small onion, diced

1 carrot, peeled and diced

1 stalk celery, diced

1 1/2 cups Chicken Stock or low-sodium chicken broth, divided

1/2 cup dried apricots, chopped

1/2 teaspoon dried thyme leaves

1/4 teaspoon kosher salt

1/8 freshly ground pepper

1/3 cup pecans, toasted and chopped

2 tablespoons chopped fresh Italian parsley

Directions:

1. Preheat the oven to 350°F. Place the bread cubes in a single layer on a large rimmed baking sheet. Bake, stirring once, until the cubes are lightly toasted, 12 to 15 minutes. Set aside. Maintain the oven temperature.

2. Brush a 2-quart baking dish with 1 teaspoon of the oil.

3. Heat a large nonstick skillet over medium heat. Add the remaining 2 teaspoons oil and tilt the pan to coat the bottom evenly. Add the onion, carrot, and celery and cook, stirring often, until the vegetables are softened, 8 minutes. Stir in 1/2 cup of the stock, the apricots, thyme, salt, and pepper and bring to a boil. Reduce the heat to low and simmer until the apricots are slightly softened, about 2 minutes.

4. Transfer the vegetable mixture to a large bowl and stir in the toasted bread cubes, pecans, and parsley. Add the remaining 1 cup stock and stir until the stock is absorbed.

5. Spoon the stuffing into the prepared baking dish, cover with foil, and bake 20 minutes. Uncover and bake until the top of the stuffing is lightly browned, about 15 minutes longer. Serve at once.

Nutrition Info:

18 g carb, 140 cal, 6 g fat, 1 g sat fat, 1 mg chol, 6 g fib, 4 g pro, 157 mg sod • Carb Choices: 1; Exchanges: 1 starch, 1 fat

Lamb Shanks Braised In Roasted Poblano Sauce

Servings: 6

Ingredients:

6 (3⁄4-pound) lamb shanks, trimmed of all visible fat

1⁄2 teaspoon kosher salt

1⁄2 teaspoon freshly ground pepper

2 teaspoons extra virgin olive oil

2 carrots, peeled and diced

2 stalks celery, diced

1 medium onion, diced

2 garlic cloves, minced

3⁄4 cup dry red wine

13⁄4 cups Beef Stock or low-sodium beef broth

1 (141⁄2-ounce) can no-salt-added diced tomatoes

4 poblano chiles, roasted and chopped

Directions:

1. Preheat the oven to 325°F.

2. Sprinkle the lamb with the salt and pepper. Heat a Dutch oven over medium-high heat. Add the oil and tilt the pot to coat the bottom evenly. Add the lamb and cook, turning often, until well browned on all sides, about 10 minutes. Transfer to a plate.

3. Add the carrots, celery, and onion to the Dutch oven and cook, stirring often, until the vegetables soften and begin to brown, 8 minutes. Add the garlic and cook, stirring constantly, until fragrant, 30 seconds. Add the wine and bring to a boil. Cook until most of the liquid evaporates, 2 minutes. Stir in the stock, tomatoes, and chiles. Return the lamb to the Dutch oven. Cover and bring to a boil. Bake until the lamb is very tender, about 2 hours.

4. Transfer the lamb to a platter and cover with foil to keep warm. Using a potato masher, mash the vegetables in the Dutch oven 4 to 5 times, until slightly mashed, but still chunky. Place the Dutch oven over medium-high heat and bring to a boil. Cook, stirring often, until the sauce is slightly thickened, about 5 minutes. Divide the lamb shanks evenly among 6 plates. Spoon the sauce evenly over the lamb and serve at once.

Nutrition Info:

10 g carb, 287 cal, 8 g fat, 3 g sat fat, 110 mg chol, 2 g fib, 36 g pro, 401 mg sod • Carb Choices: 1/2; Exchanges: 2 veg, 5 lean protein

Wild Rice with Mushrooms And Thyme

Servings: 4

Ingredients:

1/2 cup Vegetable Stock or low-sodium vegetable broth

1/2-ounce dried porcini mushrooms (about 1/2 cup)

2 teaspoons extra virgin olive oil

4 ounces shiitake mushrooms, stemmed and thinly sliced

2 shallots, minced

1/2 teaspoon kosher salt, divided 2 cups cooked wild rice

1 teaspoon chopped fresh thyme or 1/4 teaspoon dried thyme

Pinch of freshly ground pepper

Directions:

1. Bring the stock to a boil in a small saucepan. Remove from the heat, add the porcini mushrooms, cover, and let stand 30 minutes.

2. Place a coffee filter in a fine wire mesh strainer and place over a bowl. Pour the mushroom mixture through the filter. Finely chop the mushrooms and set aside and reserve the strained mushroom soaking liquid.

3. Heat a medium nonstick skillet over medium heat. Add the oil and the shiitake mushrooms, shallots, and 1/4 teaspoon of the salt and cook, stirring often, until the mushrooms are browned 8 minutes.

4. Add the reserved mushroom soaking liquid and cook until most of the liquid has evaporated, about 2 minutes. Add the porcini mushrooms, rice, thyme, remaining 1/4 teaspoon salt, and the pepper and cook, stirring often, until heated through, 2 minutes. Spoon the rice into a serving dish and serve at once.

Nutrition Info:

23 g carb, 137 cal, 3 g fat, 0 g sat fat, 0 mg chol, 3 g fib, 5 g pro, 163 mg sod • Carb Choices: 1 1/2; Exchanges: 1 1/2 starch, 1 veg, 1/2 fat

Shrimp And Spinach Pizza

Servings: 4

Ingredients:

2 teaspoons extra virgin olive oil

2 garlic cloves, minced

6 ounces medium peeled deveined shrimp

1/4 teaspoon kosher salt, divided

12 ounces fresh spinach, trimmed and chopped

1 prepared Whole Wheat Pizza Crust or 1 (12-inch) purchased prebaked whole wheat thin pizza crust

3 ounces shredded part-skim mozzarella (about 3/4 cup)

1/4 cup thinly sliced scallions

Directions:

1. Position an oven rack on the lowest rung of the oven. Preheat the oven to 450°F.

2. Heat a large nonstick skillet over medium-high heat. Add the oil and tilt the pan to coat the bottom evenly. Add the garlic and cook, stirring constantly, until fragrant, 30 seconds. Add the shrimp and 1/8 teaspoon of the salt, and cook, stirring often, just until the shrimp turn pink, about 2 minutes. Transfer to a plate.

3. Add the spinach in batches and the remaining 1/8 teaspoon salt to the skillet and cook, stirring constantly, until the spinach is wilted and most of the liquid has evaporated, about 2 minutes. Drain the spinach.

4. Place the crust on the bottom rack of the oven and bake 5 minutes.

5. Remove the crust from the oven and arrange the shrimp and the spinach evenly over the crust. Sprinkle with the mozzarella and the scallions. Bake on the bottom rack until the crust is browned and the cheese melts, about 8 minutes. Cut into 8 wedges and serve at once.

Nutrition Info:

31 g carb, 298 cal, 11 g fat, 4 g sat fat, 75 mg chol, 5 g fib, 20 g pro, 451 mg sod •
Carb Choices: 2; Exchanges: 2 starch, 1 veg, 1 high- fat protein, 1 lean protein, 1 fat

Greek Shrimp Risotto

Servings: 6

Ingredients:

4 cups Chicken Stock or low-sodium chicken broth

2 teaspoons extra virgin olive oil

1 large sweet onion, chopped

1 cup Arborio rice

2 garlic cloves, minced

1/4 teaspoon kosher salt

1/8 teaspoon freshly ground pepper

1-pound medium peeled deveined shrimp

1 medium zucchini, halved lengthwise and thinly sliced

2 ounces crumbled feta cheese (about 1/2 cup), at room temperature

2 teaspoons grated lemon zest

2 tablespoons lemon juice

1 tablespoon chopped fresh mint

1 tablespoon chopped fresh Italian parsley

Directions:

1. Pour the stock into a medium saucepan and bring to a simmer over medium-high heat. Reduce the heat to low and keep the stock warm.

2. Heat a large saucepan over medium heat. Add the oil and tilt the pan to coat the bottom evenly. Add the onion and cook, stirring often, until softened, 5 minutes. Add the rice and garlic and cook, stirring constantly, 2 minutes. Stir in the salt and pepper.

3. Add the stock, 1/2 cup at a time, stirring frequently, until the liquid is absorbed after each addition before adding more stock. When all the liquid is absorbed and the rice is tender, yet firm to the bite (about 20 minutes), add the shrimp and zucchini and cook, stirring constantly, just until the shrimp turn pink and the squash is crisp-tender, about 4 minutes.

4. Remove from the heat and stir in the feta, lemon zest, lemon juice, mint, and parsley. Spoon the risotto evenly into 6 shallow bowls and serve at once.

Nutrition Info:

32 g carb, 251 cal, 5 g fat, 2 g sat fat, 124 mg chol, 2 g fib, 20 g pro, 382 mg sod •
Carb Choices: 2; Exchanges: 2 starch, 3 lean protein, 1 fat

Chicken with Green Curry Sauce

Servings: 4

Ingredients:

3/4 cup reduced-fat coconut milk

1 teaspoon green curry paste

1 teaspoon cornstarch

4 (4-ounce) boneless skinless chicken breasts

1/2 teaspoon kosher salt

4 tablespoons chopped fresh cilantro, divided

4 teaspoons canola oil, divided

2 teaspoons minced fresh ginger

1/4 cup thinly sliced scallions

1 tablespoon lime juice

2 teaspoons Asian fish sauce

Directions:

1. Whisk together the coconut milk, curry paste, and cornstarch in a small bowl until smooth. Set aside.

2. Sprinkle the chicken with the salt, then with 2 tablespoons of the cilantro, pressing to adhere.

3. Heat a large skillet over medium heat. Add 2 teaspoons of the oil and tilt the pan to coat the bottom evenly. Add the chicken and cook, turning once, until the juices run clear, about 4 minutes on each side. Transfer to a plate and cover to keep warm.

4. Increase the heat to medium-high. Add the remaining 2 teaspoons oil and tilt the pan to coat the bottom evenly. Add the ginger and cook, stirring constantly, until fragrant, 30 seconds. Add the coconut milk mixture and the scallions and bring to a boil. Cook, stirring constantly, until the sauce is slightly thickened, about 1 minute. Remove from the heat and stir in the remaining 2 tablespoons cilantro, the lime juice, and fish sauce. Add any accumulated juices from the chicken to the skillet. Divide the chicken among 4 plates. Spoon the sauce evenly over the chicken and serve at once.

Nutrition Info:

4 g carb, 197 cal, 10 g fat, 3 g sat fat, 63 mg chol, 0 g fib, 24 g pro, 462 mg sod • Carb Choices: 0; Exchanges: 3 lean protein, 1 1/2 fat

Raspberry Pudding Cake

Servings: 10

Ingredients:

1 teaspoon plus 2 tablespoons canola oil, divided

1/2 cup granulated sugar

1/4 cup unbleached all-purpose flour

Pinch of salt

1 cup 1% low-fat buttermilk

2 teaspoons grated orange zest

1/4 cup orange juice

1 large egg yolk

2 large egg whites

1 cup fresh raspberries

1 teaspoon confectioners' sugar

Directions:

1. Preheat the oven to 350°F. Line the bottom of a 9-inch round cake pan with parchment paper. Brush the side of the pan with 1 teaspoon of the oil.

2. Combine the granulated sugar, flour, salt, buttermilk, orange zest, orange juice, egg yolk, and remaining 2 tablespoons oil in a medium bowl and whisk until the batter is smooth.

3. Place the egg whites in a medium bowl and beat at high speed with an electric mixer until stiff peaks form. Fold the egg whites into the batter in three additions, stirring until no white streaks appear. Gently stir in the raspberries. Spoon the batter into the prepared pan.

4. Place the cake pan in a large roasting pan and add hot water to the roasting pan halfway up the sides of the cake pan. Bake until the cake springs back when touched in the center and tiny cracks appear on the surface, about 35 minutes.

5. Cool the cake in the pan on a wire rack for 10 minutes. Sprinkle the top of the cake with the confectioners' sugar. Serve warm from the pan.

Nutrition Info:

16 g carb, 108 cal, 4 g fat, 1 g sat fat, 22 mg chol, 1 g fib, 2 g pro, 54 mg sod • Carb Choices: 1; Exchanges: 1 carb, 1/2 fat

Everyday Granola

Servings: 12 Cups

Ingredients:

1/2 cup honey

4 tablespoons (1/2 stick) unsalted butter

1 tablespoon ground cinnamon

1/4 teaspoon kosher salt

6 cups old-fashioned rolled oats

1/2 cup packed light brown sugar

3/4 cup sliced almonds

1/2 cup dried cranberries

Directions:

1. Preheat the oven to 350°F.

2. Combine the honey, butter, cinnamon, and salt in a medium saucepan. Bring to a boil over medium heat, stirring until the mixture is smooth.

3. Combine the oats and sugar in a large bowl. Using your fingers, evenly mix the sugar and oats. Stir in the almonds. Add the honey mixture in three additions, stirring well after each addition. Let the mixture stand until cool enough to handle, then mix thoroughly using your hands to evenly coat the oats and almonds with the honey mixture.

4. Transfer to an ungreased deep-sided roasting pan. Bake, stirring every 10 minutes, until the oats are lightly browned, 30 to 35 minutes.

5. Let stand to cool to room temperature (the granola will become crisp as it cools). Stir in the cranberries. Store the granola in an airtight container up to 1 month.

Nutrition Info:

26 g carb, 155 cal, 5 g fat, 2 g sat fat, 5 mg chol, 2 g fib, 3 g pro, 15 mg sod • Carb Choices: 2; Exchanges: 1 starch, 1 carb, 1 fat

Southern Peach Cobbler

Servings: 8

Ingredients:

1 teaspoon canola oil

FILLING

1/4 cup sugar

2 tablespoons whole wheat pastry flour or unbleached all-purpose flour

1/2 teaspoon ground cinnamon

1 teaspoon grated lemon zest

6 medium fresh peaches (about 21/2 pounds), peeled and sliced (about 6 cups) or frozen (thawed) and drained

TOPPING

3/4 cup whole wheat pastry flour or unbleached all-purpose flour

1/4 cup sugar plus 1 tablespoon sugar, divided

1/2 teaspoon baking powder

1/2 teaspoon baking soda

1/8 teaspoon salt

2 tablespoons cold unsalted butter, cut into small pieces

1/2 cup low-fat buttermilk

Directions:

1. Preheat the oven to 425°F. Brush a shallow 2-quart baking dish with the oil.

2. To make the filling, combine the sugar, flour, cinnamon, and lemon zest in a large bowl and stir to mix well. Add the peaches and toss to coat.

1. Transfer to the prepared baking dish. Bake until the fruit is bubbly around the edges, 15 to 20 minutes.

2. Meanwhile, make the topping. Combine the flour, 1/4 cup of the sugar, baking powder, baking soda, and salt in a medium bowl. Add the butter, and using a pastry blender, cut in the butter until the mixture resembles coarse meal. Add the buttermilk and stir just until the ingredients are moistened.

3. Remove the baking dish from the oven and drop the dough by 2 tablespoon measures onto the peach mixture. Sprinkle the topping with the remaining 1 tablespoon sugar. Return the cobbler to the oven and bake until the topping is lightly browned, 15 to 20 minutes. Serve warm.

Nutrition Info:

37 g carb, 190 cal, 4 g fat, 2 g sat fat, 8 mg chol, 4 g fib, 3 g pro, 157 mg sod • Carb Choices: 21/2; Exchanges: 1 1/2 carb, 1 fruit, 1/2 fat

Baked Chicken with Dried Plums And Balsamic Vinegar

Servings: 4

Ingredients:

4 (6-ounce) bone-in skin-on chicken breasts

1/2 teaspoon plus 1/8 teaspoon kosher salt, divided

1/4 teaspoon freshly ground pepper, divided

2 teaspoons extra virgin olive oil

1 1/4 cups Chicken Stock or low-sodium chicken broth

1/4 cup balsamic vinegar

1/2 cup pitted dried plums, quartered

2 garlic cloves, minced

2 tablespoons chopped fresh Italian parsley

1 teaspoon honey

Directions:

1. Preheat the oven to 375°F.

2. Gently loosen but do not detach the skin from the chicken breasts. Rub 1/2 teaspoon of the salt and 1/8 teaspoon of the pepper over the breast underneath the skin. Heat a large ovenproof skillet over medium-high heat. Add the oil and tilt the pan to coat the bottom evenly. Place the chicken in the skillet skin side down and cook until both sides are well browned, about 6 minutes.

3. Add the stock and vinegar to the skillet. Place the plums and garlic around the chicken. Transfer the skillet to the oven and bake until the juices of the chicken run clear, about 30 minutes.

4. Transfer the chicken to 4 plates. Stir the parsley, honey, remaining 1/8 teaspoon salt, and remaining 1/8 teaspoon pepper into the sauce in the skillet. Spoon the sauce evenly over the chicken. Remove the skin before eating.

Nutrition Info:

19 g carb, 240 cal, 5 g fat, 1 g sat fat, 72 mg chol, 2 g fib, 28 g pro, 274 mg sod • Carb Choices: 1; Exchanges: 1 carb, 4 lean protein, 1/2 fat

Root Vegetable Hash with Brussels Sprouts

Servings: 4

Ingredients:

2 teaspoons extra virgin olive oil

1 medium turnip, peeled and chopped

1 parsnip, peeled and sliced

1 carrot, peeled and sliced

1 small red onion, halved and thinly sliced

3⁄4 teaspoon kosher salt

Pinch of freshly ground pepper

1 cup Brussels sprouts, trimmed and quartered

1 garlic clove, minced

Directions:

1. Heat a large nonstick skillet over medium-high heat. Add the oil and tilt the pan to coat the bottom evenly.

2. Add the turnip, parsnip, carrot, onion, salt, and pepper and stir to coat. Cook, stirring occasionally, until the vegetables are lightly browned, about 5 minutes. Reduce the heat to medium, cover, and cook, stirring occasionally, until the vegetables are almost tender, about 5 minutes. Add the Brussels sprouts and garlic, cover, and cook, stirring occasionally, until all the vegetables are tender, 3 to 5 minutes longer. Spoon the hash into a serving dish and serve hot or warm.

Nutrition Info:

14 g carb, 83 cal, 3 g fat, 0 g sat fat, 0 mg chol, 4 g fib, 2 g pro, 347 mg sod • Carb Choices: 1; Exchanges: 3 veg, 1/2 fat

Shrimp And Black Bean Soup with Chile And Lime

vServings: 6

Ingredients:

3 (6-inch) corn tortillas, cut in half, then into thin strips

2 teaspoons extra virgin olive oil

1 large onion, diced

1 green bell pepper, diced

1 jalapeño, seeded and minced

2 garlic cloves, minced

1 tablespoon ground cumin

4 1/2 cups Shrimp Stock or 3 1/2 cups Chicken Stock or low-sodium chicken broth plus 1 (8-ounce) bottle clam juice

1 (14 1/2 ounce) can no-salt-added diced tomatoes

1 (15-ounce) can no-salt-added black beans, rinsed and drained

1-pound medium peeled deveined shrimp

2 tablespoons lime juice

1/2 cup chopped fresh cilantro

Directions:

1. Preheat the oven to 350°F. Place the tortilla strips on a baking sheet and bake until crisp, 10 minutes.

2. Meanwhile, heat a large pot over medium heat. Add the oil and tilt the pot to coat the bottom evenly. Add the onion, bell pepper, and jalapeño and cook, stirring often, until softened, 5 minutes. Add the garlic and cumin and cook, stirring constantly, until fragrant, 30 seconds.

3. Add the stock, tomatoes, and beans and bring to a boil. Cover, reduce the heat to low, and simmer until the vegetables are tender, about 15 minutes. Stir in the shrimp and cook until the shrimp turn pink, about 2 minutes. Remove from the heat and stir in the lime juice and cilantro. Ladle into 6 bowls, top evenly with the tortilla strips, and serve at once. The soup is best on the day it is made.

Nutrition Info:

23 g carb, 193 cal, 3 g fat, 0 g sat fat, 113 mg chol, 6 g fib, 19 g pro, 328 mg sod • Carb Choices: 1 1/2; Exchanges: 1 starch, 1 veg, 1 1/2 lean protein

Broiled Fish Fillets with Chipotle And Lime

Servings: 4

Ingredients:

1/2 teaspoon canola oil

4 (5-ounce) thin white-fleshed fish fillets

1 teaspoon grated lime zest

1/2 teaspoon chipotle chile powder

1/4 teaspoon kosher salt

Lime wedges

Directions:

1. Preheat the broiler. Brush a medium rimmed baking sheet with the oil.

2. Sprinkle the fish with the lime zest, chile powder, and salt and arrange in a single layer on the prepared baking sheet. Broil, without turning, until the fish flakes easily with a fork, about 8 minutes. Transfer the fish to 4 plates using a wide spatula and serve at once with the lime wedges.

Nutrition Info:

0 g carb, 120 cal, 2 g fat, 0 g sat fat, 67 mg chol, 0 g fib, 24 g pro, 173 mg sod •
Carb Choices: 0; Exchanges: 3 lean protein

Asian Dipping Sauce

Servings: 1/3 Cup

Ingredients:

2 tablespoons Asian fish sauce

2 tablespoons lime juice

2 tablespoons cold water

1 teaspoon sugar

1 garlic clove, crushed through a press

1/2 jalapeño or other small hot chile, minced

Directions:

1. Combine all the ingredients in a small bowl and stir until the sugar dissolves. The sauce can be refrigerated, covered, for up to 4 days.

Nutrition Info:

1 g carb, 5 cal, 0 g fat, 0 g sat fat, 0 mg chol, 0 g fib, 0 g pro, 348 mg sod • Carb Choices: 0

Vegetable Stock

Servings: 8 Cups

Ingredients:

12 cups cold water

2 large carrots, peeled and cut into 1-inch chunks

2 stalks celery, cut into 1-inch chunks

1 large onion, chopped

4 sprigs Italian parsley

2 garlic cloves, smashed

8 black peppercorns

2 bay leaves

1 teaspoon kosher salt

Directions:

1. Combine all the ingredients in a large pot. Bring just to a simmer over medium heat. Reduce the heat to low and simmer, partially covered, with bubbles gently coming to the surface in the center of the pot, 1 hour.

2. Place a colander in a large bowl and pour in the stock. Discard the vegetables and seasonings. Use the stock at once or let stand to cool to room temperature. The cooled stock can be refrigerated, covered, for up to 4 days or frozen for up to 6 months.

Nutrition Info:

2 g carb, 10 cal, 0 g fat, 0 g sat fat, 0 mg chol, 0 g fib, 0 g pro, 70 mg sod • Carb Choices: 0; Exchanges: None

Grilled Sweet Onion Slices with Sherry Vinegar And Thyme

Servings: 4

Ingredients:

1 large sweet onion

2 1/2 teaspoons extra virgin olive oil, divided

2 teaspoons sherry vinegar or red wine vinegar

1 teaspoon chopped fresh thyme or 1/4 teaspoon dried thyme

1/2 teaspoon kosher salt

Pinch of freshly ground pepper

Directions:

1. Prepare the grill or heat a large grill pan over medium-high heat.

2. Cut a thin slice off the stem and root end of the onion and discard. Peel the onion and cut into 4 slices.

3. Brush the onion slices with 2 teaspoons of the oil. Brush the grill rack or grill pan with the remaining 1/2 teaspoon oil. Place the onions on the grill rack or in the grill pan and grill, turning once using a wide spatula to prevent the rings from separating, until the onions are tender, 8 to 10 minutes.

4. To serve, arrange the onions on a serving platter. Drizzle with the vinegar, sprinkle with the thyme, salt, and pepper. Serve hot, warm, or at room temperature.

Nutrition Info:

6 g carb, 54 cal, 3 g fat, 0 g sat fat, 0 mg chol, 1 g fib, 1 g pro, 147 mg sod • Carb Choices: 1/2; Exchanges: 1 veg, 1/2 fat

Parmesan Popcorn

Servings: 4

Ingredients:

2 teaspoons canola oil

1/4 cup popcorn kernels

3 tablespoons freshly grated Parmesan

1/8 teaspoon salt

Directions:

1. Heat a large saucepan over medium heat. Add the oil and tilt the pan to coat the bottom evenly. Add 4 or 5 popcorn kernels and cover the pan. When the kernels pop, add the remaining popcorn kernels and tilt the pan to coat the kernels. Cover the pan and cook until the popping stops, about 3 minutes.

2. Transfer the popcorn to a large serving bowl. Immediately sprinkle with the Parmesan and the salt and toss to coat. Serve at once.

Nutrition Info:

10 g carb, 87 cal, 4 g fat, 1 g sat fat, 3 mg chol, 2 g fib, 3 g pro, 131 mg sod • Carb Choices: 1/2; Exchanges: 1/2 starch, 1/2 fat

Roasted Sweet Potatoes with Ginger And Lime

Servings: 4

Ingredients:

2 medium sweet potatoes (about 1 pound)

2 teaspoons extra virgin olive oil

1/4 teaspoon kosher salt

1 tablespoon lime juice

1 teaspoon grated fresh ginger

Directions:

1. Preheat the oven to 425°F.
2. Peel the potatoes and cut each into 8 wedges. Place the potatoes on a large rimmed baking sheet. Drizzle with the oil and sprinkle with the salt. Toss to coat. Arrange in a single layer.
3. Roast, turning the potatoes once, until tender and browned, 30 to 35 minutes.
4. Stir together the lime juice and ginger in a small bowl. To serve, arrange the potatoes on a serving platter, drizzle with the lime mixture, and turn to coat. Serve hot or warm.

Nutrition Info:

15 g carb, 84 cal, 2 g fat, 0 g sat fat, 0 mg chol, 2 g fib, 1 g pro, 95 mg sod • Carb Choices: 1; Exchanges: 1 starch, 1/2 fat

Tri-color Salad

Servings: 4

Ingredients:

1 canned anchovy fillet, drained

1 1/2 tablespoons extra virgin olive oil

1 tablespoon balsamic vinegar

1 garlic clove, crushed through a press

1/4 teaspoon kosher salt

1/4 teaspoon freshly ground pepper

4 cups loosely packed torn romaine lettuce

4 cups loosely packed torn radicchio

1 head Belgian endive, torn

1/4 cup shaved Parmesan

Directions:

1. Place the anchovy in a large bowl and use two forks to mash it into a paste. Add the oil, vinegar, garlic, salt, and pepper and whisk until smooth.
2. Add the romaine, radicchio, and endive and toss to coat. Divide the salad among 4 plates and sprinkle evenly with the Parmesan. Serve at once.

Nutrition Info:

5 g carb, 96 cal, 7 g fat, 2 g sat fat, 4 mg chol, 2 g fib, 4 g pro, 206 mg sod • Carb Choices: 0; Exchanges: 1 veg, 1 fat

Slow-cooking Steel-cut Oatmeal

Servings: 4

Ingredients:

3 cups water

Pinch of kosher salt

3⁄4 cup steel-cut oats

Directions:

1. Combine the water and salt in a medium saucepan and bring to a boil over medium-high heat. Slowly stir in the oats and return to a boil.
2. Reduce the heat to low, and simmer, uncovered, stirring occasionally, until the oats are tender, 20 to 25 minutes. Depending on how chewy you prefer your oats, you may need to add a little more water and cook them 5 to 10 minutes longer.

Nutrition Info:

20 g carb, 111 cal, 2 g fat, 0 g sat fat, 0 mg chol, 3 g fib, 4 g pro, 18 mg sod • Carb Choices: 1; Exchanges: 1 starch

Barley Risotto with Mushrooms And Gorgonzola

Servings: 4

Ingredients:

4 1/2 cups Vegetable Stock or low-sodium vegetable broth

2 teaspoons extra virgin olive oil

8 ounces cremini mushrooms, thinly sliced

1 medium onion, diced

2 garlic cloves, minced

3/4 cup pearl barley

1/2 cup dry white wine

1/2 teaspoon kosher salt

3 tablespoons crumbled Gorgonzola or other blue cheese

1 teaspoon fresh minced thyme or 1/4 teaspoon dried thyme

1/8 teaspoon freshly ground pepper

Directions:

1.   Pour the stock into a medium saucepan and bring to a simmer over medium-high heat. Reduce the heat to low and keep the stock warm.

2.   Heat a large saucepan over medium heat. Add the oil and tilt the pan to coat the bottom evenly. Add the mushrooms and onion and cook, stirring often, until the mushrooms are tender and most of the liquid has evaporated, about 8 minutes. Add the garlic and cook, stirring constantly, until fragrant, 30 seconds.

3.   Add the barley and cook, stirring constantly, 2 minutes. Add the wine and salt and cook, stirring frequently, until the liquid is absorbed. Add the stock, 1/2 cup at a time, stirring frequently, until the liquid is absorbed after each addition before adding more stock.

4.   When all the liquid is absorbed and the barley is tender (about 35 minutes), remove the saucepan from the heat and stir in the Gorgonzola, thyme, and pepper. Spoon the risotto evenly into 4 shallow bowls and serve at once.

Nutrition Info:

39 g carb, 247 cal, 4 g fat, 2 g sat fat, 5 mg chol, 7 g fib, 6 g pro, 377 mg sod • Carb Choices: 2; Exchanges: 2 starch, 1 veg, 1 fat

Pasta with Beef And Mushroom Bolognese Sauce

Servings: 6

Ingredients:

12 ounces 95% lean ground beef, crumbled

8 ounces cremini or white mushrooms, sliced

1 medium onion, diced

1 carrot, peeled and diced

1 stalk celery, diced

2 garlic cloves, minced

1/2 cup dry red wine

1 (28-ounce) can no-salt-added whole tomatoes, undrained and chopped

2 tablespoons no-salt-added tomato paste

1/2 teaspoon kosher salt

1/4 teaspoon freshly ground pepper

1/4 cup chopped fresh basil

12 ounces whole wheat fettuccini or spaghetti

3 tablespoons freshly grated Parmesan

Directions:

1.Combine the beef, mushrooms, onion, carrot, celery, and garlic in a large nonstick skillet and cook over medium-high heat, stirring often, until the beef is browned, about 8 minutes.

2.Stir in the wine and cook, stirring often, until almost all the liquid is absorbed, 2 minutes. Add the tomatoes with their juice, tomato paste, salt, and pepper and bring to a boil. Reduce the heat to low and simmer,

uncovered, until the vegetables are tender and the sauce is thickened, 15 to 20 minutes. Stir in the basil during the last 5 minutes of cooking.

3.Meanwhile, cook the pasta according to the package directions. Divide the pasta among 6 shallow bowls and top evenly with the sauce. Sprinkle evenly with the Parmesan and serve at once. You can make a double batch of the sauce and freeze half for up to 3 months.

Nutrition Info:

52 g carb, 329 cal, 5 g fat, 2 g sat fat, 37 mg chol, 9 g fib, 24 g pro, 212 mg sod •
Carb Choices: 3; Exchanges: 2½ starch, 2 veg, 2 lean protein

Shrimp Stock

Servings: 8 Cups

Ingredients:

Shells from 1 pound of shrimp

10 cups cold water

1 large onion, chopped

2 large carrots, peeled and cut into 1-inch chunks

2 stalks celery, cut into 1-inch chunks

4 sprigs Italian parsley

2 garlic cloves, smashed

8 black peppercorns

2 bay leaves

1 teaspoon kosher salt

Directions:

1. Combine all the ingredients in a large pot. Bring just to a simmer over medium heat. Reduce the heat to low and simmer, partially covered, with bubbles gently coming to the surface in the center of the pot, 45 minutes. Do not stir the stock while it cooks.

2. Place a colander in a large bowl and pour in the stock. Discard the shells, vegetables, and seasonings. Strain the stock through a fine wire mesh strainer.

3. Let stand to cool to room temperature. Use the stock at once or refrigerate, covered, for up to 4 days or freeze for up to 3 months.

Nutrition Info:

1 g carb, 19 cal, 0 g fat, 0 g sat fat, 0 mg chol, 0 g fib, 2 g pro, 70 mg sod • Carb Choices: 0; Exchanges: None

Panko-crusted Chicken

Servings: 4

Ingredients:

1/2 teaspoon plus 2 teaspoons extra virgin olive oil, divided

3 tablespoons unbleached all-purpose flour

1 large egg white

1 tablespoon Dijon mustard

1 tablespoon water

3/4 cup panko crumbs

1 ounce freshly grated Parmesan (about 1/4 cup)

4 (4-ounce) boneless skinless chicken breasts

1/2 teaspoon kosher salt

1/8 teaspoon freshly ground pepper

Directions:

1. Position an oven rack in the top third of the oven. Preheat the oven to 375°F. Brush a medium rimmed baking sheet with 1/2 teaspoon of the oil.

2. Place the flour in a shallow dish. Place the egg white, mustard, and water in another shallow dish and beat lightly with a fork. Combine the panko crumbs, Parmesan, and the remaining 2 teaspoons oil in another shallow dish. Using your fingers, blend the oil evenly into the crumbs.

3. Sprinkle the chicken with the salt and pepper. Dip the chicken, one piece at a time into the flour, then into the egg white mixture, then into the crumb mixture, pressing to adhere the crumbs.

4. Arrange the chicken in a single layer on the prepared baking sheet. Bake until the juices of the chicken run clear, 20 minutes (do not turn). Turn on the broiler and broil the chicken until the crust is lightly browned, 1 to 2 minutes. Divide the chicken among 4 plates and serve at once.

Nutrition Info:

14 g carb, 236 cal, 7 g fat, 2 g sat fat, 67 mg chol, 0 g fib, 28 g pro, 400 mg sod • Carb Choices: 1; Exchanges: 1 starch, 3 lean protein, 1 fat

Yogurt-and-brown-sugar-glazed Fruit

Servings: 4

Ingredients:

4 large plums, pitted and quartered

1 cup fresh blueberries or frozen unsweetened blueberries, thawed

1/3 cup plain low-fat yogurt

1 teaspoon vanilla extract

2 tablespoons light brown sugar

Directions:

1. Preheat the broiler.

2. Place the plums and blueberries in a shallow flameproof baking pan and toss to combine.

3. Stir together the yogurt and vanilla in a small bowl. Spoon the mixture over the fruit and sprinkle with the sugar.

4. Broil until the fruit is warmed and the sugar is lightly browned, about 5 minutes. Serve at once.

Nutrition Info:

24 g carb, 103 cal, 0 g fat, 0 g sat fat, 1 mg chol, 2 g fib, 2 g pro, 17 mg sod • Carb Choices: 1½; Exchanges: ½ carb, 1 fruit

Stir-fried Broccoli with Ginger Sauce

Servings: 4

Ingredients:

2 tablespoons Chicken Stock or low-sodium chicken broth

1 teaspoon reduced-sodium soy sauce

1 teaspoon hoisin sauce 1/4 teaspoon cornstarch

2 teaspoons canola oil

2 teaspoons minced fresh ginger

1 garlic clove, minced

3 cups broccoli florets, cut into bite-size pieces

Directions:

1. Stir together the stock, soy sauce, hoisin sauce, and cornstarch in a small bowl and set aside.

2. Heat a large nonstick skillet over medium-high heat. Add the oil and tilt the pan to coat the bottom evenly. Add the ginger and garlic and cook, stirring constantly, until fragrant, 30 seconds.

3. Add the broccoli and cook, stirring constantly, until the broccoli is crisp-tender, 3 minutes. Stir the stock mixture and add to the skillet. Cook, stirring constantly, until the sauce comes to a boil and thickens slightly, 1 minute. Spoon the broccoli and sauce into a serving dish and serve at once.

Nutrition Info:

4 g carb, 43 cal, 3 g fat, 0 g sat fat, 0 mg chol, 2 g fib, 2 g pro, 91 mg sod • Carb Choices: 0; Exchanges: 1 veg, 1/2 fat

Beef Bourguignon

Servings: 8

Ingredients:

2 strips center-cut bacon, coarsely chopped

2 pounds beef chuck shoulder roast or bottom round roast, trimmed of all visible fat and cut into 1-inch cubes

2 tablespoons unbleached all-purpose flour

1 teaspoon kosher salt

1/4 teaspoon freshly ground pepper

2 teaspoons extra virgin olive oil

1 medium onion, chopped

1 stalk celery, chopped

2 garlic cloves, minced

1/3 cup brandy

2 cups dry red wine

2 tablespoons no-salt-added tomato paste

8 ounces pearl onions or small boiling onions

1 pound small whole white or cremini mushrooms

2 tablespoons chopped fresh Italian parsley

Directions:

1. Preheat the oven to 325°F.

2. Cook the bacon in a Dutch oven over medium-high heat until crisp. Drain on paper towels and set aside. Pour off all but 2 teaspoons of the drippings into a small bowl. Reserve the drippings.

3. Place the beef in a large bowl. Sprinkle with the flour, salt, and pepper and toss to coat. Add half of the beef to the Dutch oven and cook over medium heat, turning occasionally, until well browned, about 6 minutes. Transfer the beef to a plate. Repeat with the reserved bacon drippings and beef.

4. Add the oil to the Dutch oven and tilt the pot to coat the bottom evenly. Add the onion and celery and cook, stirring often, until softened, about 5 minutes. Add the garlic and cook, stirring constantly, until fragrant, 30 seconds.

5. Add the brandy and bring to a boil, stirring to scrape up the browned bits in the bottom of the pot. Add the bacon, beef, wine, and tomato paste and bring to a boil. Cover and bake 2 hours.

6. Meanwhile, bring a medium saucepan of water to a boil. Add the pearl onions and cook 1 minute. Drain in a colander and rinse with cold running water. Peel the onions, leaving the roots intact (the skins will slip off easily after boiling).

7. Remove the Dutch oven from the oven and stir in the onions and mushrooms. Bake until the beef is very tender, 1 hour longer. Stir in the parsley just before serving. Divide the stew evenly among 8 shallow bowls and serve at once.

Nutrition Info:

10 g carb, 283 cal, 9 g fat, 3 g sat fat, 53 mg chol, 1 g fib, 24 g pro, 238 mg sod • Carb Choices: 1/2; Exchanges: 1 veg, 3 lean protein, 1 fat

Chocolate Brownies

Servings: 16

Ingredients:

1 teaspoon plus 1/2 cup (1 stick) unsalted butter, softened, divided

1/2 cup unbleached all-purpose flour

1/2 cup unsweetened cocoa

1/2 teaspoon baking powder

1/4 teaspoon salt

1 tablespoon hot water

1/2 teaspoon instant espresso granules

1 cup sugar

2 egg whites

1 large egg

1 teaspoon vanilla extract

Directions:

1. Preheat the oven to 350°F. Line an 8-inch square metal baking pan with foil, allowing the foil to extend over the rim of the pan by 2 inches. Brush the foil with 1 teaspoon of the butter.

2. Combine the flour, cocoa, baking powder, and salt in a medium bowl and whisk to mix well.

3. Combine the hot water and espresso granules in a small dish and stir until the espresso dissolves.

4. Place the remaining 1/2 cup butter in a large bowl and beat at medium speed with an electric mixer until fluffy. Gradually beat in the sugar. Beat in the egg whites, egg, vanilla, and espresso mixture. Add the flour mixture and beat at low speed just until the batter is moistened.

5. Spoon the batter into the prepared pan and spread evenly. Bake until a wooden toothpick inserted into the center comes out clean, 20 to 23 minutes. (Be careful not to overbake. The center of the brownies should still be soft.) Cool completely in pan on a wire rack. Lift from the pan using the foil overhang as handles. Cut into 16 squares. The brownies can be stored in an airtight container at room temperature for up to 3 days.

Nutrition Info:1 7 g carb, 127 cal, 7 g fat, 4 g sat fat, 29 mg chol, 1 g fib, 2 g pro, 62 mg sod • Carb Choices: 1; Exchanges: 1 carb, 1 fat

Roast Chicken with Vegetables

Servings: 6

Ingredients:

1 whole chicken (about 3 1/4 pounds)

2 garlic cloves, minced

3/4 teaspoon kosher salt, divided

1/2 teaspoon freshly ground pepper, divided

12 ounces green beans, trimmed

8 ounces baby potatoes, well scrubbed and quartered

8 ounces carrots, peeled and cut into 1/2-inch-thick sticks

2 teaspoons extra virgin olive oil

Directions:

1. Preheat the oven to 400°F.

2. Remove and discard the neck and giblets from the cavity of the chicken. Loosen the skin from the breast and drumsticks by inserting your fingers and gently separating the skin from the meat. Rub the garlic, 1/2 teaspoon of the salt, and 1/4 teaspoon of the pepper over the breast and drumsticks underneath the skin.

3. Place the chicken in a large roasting pan. Bake 15 minutes.

4. Meanwhile, combine the green beans, potatoes, carrots, oil, remaining 1/4 teaspoon salt, and remaining 1/4 teaspoon pepper in a large bowl and toss to coat. Arrange the vegetables around the chicken. Continue roasting, stirring the vegetables once, until an instant-read thermometer inserted into a thigh reads 165°F, 45 minutes to 1 hour.

5. Transfer the chicken to a platter, cover loosely with foil, and let stand 10 minutes before carving.

6. Carve the chicken and divide the chicken and vegetables evenly among 6 plates. Remove the skin from the chicken before eating.

Nutrition Info:

14 g carb, 213 cal, 5 g fat, 1 g sat fat, 81 mg chol, 4 g fib, 28 g pro, 263 mg sod •
Carb Choices: 1; Exchanges: 1/2 starch, 1 veg, 4 lean protein

Roasted Garlic Eggplant Dip

Servings: 1 1/2 Cups

Ingredients:

1 large eggplant (about 1½ pounds)

1 teaspoon extra virgin olive oil

1 head of garlic

3 tablespoons lemon juice

2 tablespoons tahini (sesame paste)

2 tablespoons chopped fresh Italian parsley or basil

3/4 teaspoon kosher salt

Directions:

1. Preheat the oven to 375°F.

2. Cut the eggplant in half lengthwise and brush the cut side with the oil. Place the eggplant cut side down on a medium rimmed baking sheet. Wrap the garlic in a sheet of foil and place on the baking sheet.

3. Bake until the eggplant and the garlic are very tender, about 1 hour. Let stand to cool to room temperature.

4. Scoop out the eggplant flesh and squeeze the pulp from each garlic clove. Combine the eggplant, garlic, lemon juice, tahini, parsley, and salt in a food processor and process until smooth. The dip can be refrigerated, covered, for up to 3 days. Bring to room temperature before serving.

Nutrition Info:

9 g carb, 68 cal, 4 g fat, 1 g sat fat, 0 mg chol, 4 g fib, 2 g pro, 145 mg sod • Carb Choices: 1/2; Exchanges: 1 veg, 1/2 fat

Vietnamese Banh Mi

Servings: 4

Ingredients:

3 tablespoons sugar, divided

2 tablespoons lime juice

2 tablespoons Asian fish sauce

2 garlic cloves, chopped

1 scallion, chopped

1 tablespoon chopped fresh ginger

1 (1-pound) pork tenderloin, trimmed of all visible fat

1/2 cup rice vinegar

1/4 teaspoon kosher salt

1 carrot, peeled and cut into thin matchstick strips

1 daikon radish or 1 small jicama, peeled and cut into thin matchstick strips

1 jalapeño, halved lengthwise, seeded, and thinly sliced

2 teaspoons canola oil

4 (6-inch) whole wheat baguettes, split and toasted

2 tablespoons mayonnaise

1/2 cup loosely packed cilantro leaves

Directions:

1. Combine the 1 tablespoon of the sugar, the lime juice, fish sauce, garlic, scallion, and ginger in a large resealable plastic bag. Add the pork and turn to coat. Seal the bag and refrigerate 4 hours and up to 8 hours, turning the bag occasionally.

2. Combine the vinegar, remaining 2 tablespoons sugar, and salt in a small saucepan and bring to a boil over high heat, stirring to dissolve the sugar. Place the carrot, daikon, and jalapeño in a medium bowl. Add the vinegar mixture and toss to coat. Cover and refrigerate until ready to serve.

3. Preheat the oven to 400°F.

4. Remove the pork from the bag and discard the marinade. Pat the pork dry with paper towels.

5. Heat a large ovenproof skillet over medium-high heat until hot. Add the oil and tilt the pan to coat the bottom evenly. Add the tenderloin and cook, until browned on all sides, about 5 minutes. Transfer to the oven and bake, turning once, until an instant-read thermometer inserted into the center reads 145°F, 15 to 20 minutes. Cover with foil and let stand 10 minutes. Cut into thin slices.

6. To serve, spread the cut sides of the baguettes evenly with the mayonnaise. Drain the daikon mixture. Divide the pork among the baguettes and top evenly with the daikon mixture and cilantro leaves. Serve at once.

Nutrition Info:

22 g carb, 316 cal, 14 g fat, 2 g sat fat, 66 mg chol, 3 g fib, 27 g pro, 638 mg sod • Carb Choices: 1 1/2; Exchanges: 1 1/2 starch, 3 lean protein, 2 1/2 fat

Crustless Asparagus And Feta Tart

Servings: 6

Ingredients:

1/2 teaspoon canola oil

1 1/2 pounds asparagus, tough ends removed and spears cut into 3/4-inch pieces (about 3 cups)

4 large eggs

4 large egg whites

3/4 cup 1% low-fat milk

2 tablespoons unbleached all-purpose flour

1 garlic clove, crushed through a press

1/2 teaspoon kosher salt

1/4 teaspoon freshly ground pepper

4 ounces finely crumbled feta cheese (about 1 cup)

Directions:

1. Preheat the oven to 350°F. Brush a 9- or 10-inch ceramic quiche pan or a 10-inch glass or ceramic pie plate with the oil.

2. Bring a large saucepan of water to a boil over high heat. Add the asparagus and cook until crisp-tender, 3 to 4 minutes. Drain in a colander and rinse with cold running water until cool. Pat the asparagus dry with paper towels.

3. Combine the eggs, egg whites, milk, flour, garlic, salt, and pepper in a large bowl and whisk until smooth. Add the asparagus and the feta and stir to combine. Pour into the prepared pan and arrange the asparagus evenly.

4. Place the quiche pan on a large rimmed baking sheet. Bake until the top is golden and the center is set, 30 to 35 minutes. Let stand 5 minutes. Cut the tart into 6 wedges using a serrated knife. Serve hot, warm, or at room temperature.

Nutrition Info:

7 g carb, 153 cal, 8 g fat, 4 g sat fat, 159 mg chol, 1 g fib, 12 g pro, 407 mg sod • Carb Choices: 1/2; Exchanges: 1 veg, 1 medium-fat protein, 1 fat

Chicken And Peanut Stew

Servings: 6

Ingredients:

1-pound boneless skinless chicken thighs, cut into 1/2-inch pieces

1/2 teaspoon kosher salt

2 teaspoons extra virgin olive oil

2 tablespoons minced fresh ginger

2 garlic cloves, minced

3 cups Chicken Stock or low-sodium chicken broth

2 medium sweet potatoes (about 1 pound), peeled and chopped

2 carrots, peeled and chopped

1 (141/2-ounce) can no-salt added diced tomatoes

1 jalapeño pepper, chopped

1/8 teaspoon ground cayenne

1/4 cup natural creamy peanut butter

4 cups chopped fresh spinach

2 tablespoons lime juice

Directions:

1. Sprinkle the chicken with the salt. Heat a large saucepan over medium- high heat. Add the oil and tilt the pan to coat the bottom evenly. Add the chicken and cook, stirring often, until well browned, about 8 minutes. Add the ginger and garlic and cook, stirring constantly, until fragrant, 30 seconds.

2. Add the stock, sweet potatoes, carrots, tomatoes, jalapeño, and cayenne and bring to a boil. Cover, reduce the heat to low, and simmer until the vegetables are tender, about 25 minutes. Add the peanut butter and cook, stirring often, until smooth. Stir in the spinach and cook just until wilted, 2 minutes. Stir in the lime juice. Ladle the stew evenly into 6 bowls and serve at once. The stew can be refrigerated, covered, for up to 4 days.

Nutrition Info:

20 g carb, 283 cal, 13 g fat, 3 g sat fat, 53 mg chol, 4 g fib, 21 g pro, 333 mg sod •
Carb Choices: 1; Exchanges: 1 starch, 1 veg, 2 lean protein, 1 1/2 fat

Beets with Sautéed Beet Greens

Servings: 6

Ingredients:

1 1/2 pounds beets with green tops attached

2 teaspoons extra virgin olive oil

1/2 small onion, thinly sliced

1 garlic clove, minced

1/2 cup Vegetable Stock or low-sodium vegetable broth

1/4 teaspoon kosher salt

1/2 teaspoon red wine vinegar

Directions:

1. Thinly slice the tops of the beets and set aside. Prepare the beets using either the recipe for Foil-Roasted Beets (above) or Basic Boiled Beets (above). Cut the beets into bite-size pieces.

2. Heat a large nonstick skillet over medium heat. Add the oil and tilt the pan to coat the bottom evenly. Add the onion and cook, stirring often, until softened, 5 minutes. Add the garlic and cook, stirring constantly, 30 seconds.

3. Add the stock and the beet greens and cook, stirring often, until the greens are tender, 5 minutes.

4. Add the beets and salt and cook, stirring often, until heated through, about 3 minutes. Remove from the heat and stir in the vinegar. Spoon the beets into a serving dish and serve at once.

Nutrition Info:

7 g carb, 47 cal, 2 g fat, 0 g sat fat, 0 mg chol, 2 g fib, 2 g pro, 158 mg sod • Carb Choices: 1/2; Exchanges: 1 veg, 1/2 fat

Alphabetical Index

V

W

Y

CPSIA information can be obtained
at www.ICGtesting.com
Printed in the USA
BVHW041518030621
608739BV00002B/555